Tariq's Big Trip

Mini Mu'min Du'a Series #15

www.Mini-Mumin.com

Copyright © 2012 Mini Mu'min Publications

All rights reserved. This publication may not be reproduced in whole or in part by any means whatsoever without written permission from the copyright owner.

Introduction

All praise is due to Allah the Most High, may Allah send His blessings on the Prophet Muhammad (saw), his family, his companions, and those who follow him in righteousness until the Day of Judgment.

"And remember your Lord by your tongue and within yourself, humbly and in awe, without loudness, by words in the morning and the afternoon, and be not among those who are neglectful." (Holy Qur'an 7:205)

The **Mini Mu'min Du'a Series** is designed to help you teach your child essential Islamic supplications and the situations in which they would be used. Each book focuses on a single topic, with key vocabulary highlighted. These key words can then serve as a tool to remind your child of important points. All supplications are shown in Arabic text, translation, and transliteration. For any assertions regarding fiqh we have provided textual proofs, from the Qur'an and authentic Sunnah of the Prophet (saw), at the bottom of the relevant page. Each story is accompanied by original artwork, but in accordance with Islamic beliefs we do not use human or animal images.

Transliteration has been provided here as a means to help those who do not know Arabic to teach supplications to their children. But it must be noted that all transliteration is imperfect and cannot accurately represent Arabic sounds in their entirety. We therefore encourage anyone who uses our books to use the transliteration as a tool, but not an end in itself, and to eventually learn the supplications in the original Arabic.

In some cases, sounds will be represented in the transliteration (because they are present in the Arabic text) that will not actually be pronounced. These generally occur at the end of a supplication and are related to the Arabic rules for pausing and stopping. To clarify this for non-Arabic speakers, we have placed brackets [ ] around those sounds in the transliteration that would not be pronounced when reciting the supplication.

Thank you for purchasing this book, may Allah benefit both you and your child through it, forgive us for any errors we have made, and benefit us in this life and the Hereafter if there is any good in it.

There are lots of places to travel,
There are all kinds of interesting trips-

You can travel around the whole world
In planes, trains, buses, and ships!

This is Tariq's first BIG trip ever,
A long journey over land and sea-

To visit a new country for the first time,
And meet his father's whole family!

Tariq's family is traveling together,
They don't like to travel **alone**,[1]

Because it's very hard for a person
To be **far away from their home**.[2]

His mother, father, and sister are going-
Tariq and his brother are coming, too…

It's so nice when your entire family
Can travel along with you!

---

[1] Ibn 'Umar (ra) reported: The Messenger of Allah (saw) said, "Were people to know what I know about the dangers of traveling alone, no rider would travel alone at night." (Al-Bukhaari)

[2] Abu Huraira (ra) reported: The Messenger of Allah (saw) said, "Traveling is a torment because it deprives a traveler of his food, drink, and sleep. So when one of you has accomplished his purpose of journey, let him return home quickly." (Al-Bukhaari and Muslim)

This is Tariq's first time traveling,
There's a lot he doesn't know.

He keeps asking all kinds of questions,
So he will be ready before they go…

"How long will it take to get there?"
"When will we be coming back?"

"What will we do while we're there?"
"Should I bring along a snack?"

"Hold on a minute," said Tariq's father,
"We're not ready to leave just yet-

There are a couple of important things
We need to be sure that we don't forget…"

"You mean things like soap and a towel;
A toothbrush and plenty of clothes?"

"Don't worry," said Tariq with a smile,
"I remembered to pack all of those!"

"Great job!" said Tariq's father,
"But I didn't mean those kinds of things-

I'm not talking about what we pack,
Or the stuff that a traveler brings...

I'm talking about the special adi'yaa[3]
That the Muslim always makes,

When he leaves, and when he returns,
From each and every journey he takes."

---

[3] Note: There are a large number of supplications related to traveling, here we have focused on four key supplications as a child's introduction to the topic. For more supplications related to travel see our Du'a Series title- <u>Rasheed's Family Goes for a Ride</u>.

"**Before you leave** on your trip,
There's a du'a that you say,

Asking Allah to protect your **family**
And your **friends** while you are away..."

أَسْتَوْدِعُكُمُ اللهَ الَّذِي لاَ تَضِيعُ وَدَائِعُهُ

"*Astawdi'ukumul-laahal-la<u>th</u>ee
laa tadhee'u wadaa'i'uh[u]*"

(I leave you in the care of Allah,
as nothing is lost that is in His care.)[4]

---

[4] Supplication of the Traveler for the Resident (Ahmad 2/403 and Ibn Maajah 2/943, see also: *Sahih Ibn Maajah* 2/133).

"Then, the **people staying behind**
Have a special du'a to make, too...

They respond by asking Allah,
To **protect** and take care of **you**..."

أَسْتَوْدِعُ اللهَ دِينَكَ، وَأَمَانَتَكَ،
وَ خَوَاتِيمَ عَمَلِكَ

"Astawdi'ullaaha deenaka,
wa amaa-nataka, wa
khawaateema 'amalik[a]"

(I leave your religion in the care
of Allah, as well as your safety,
and the last of your deeds.)[5]

---

[5] Supplication of the Resident for the Traveler (Ahmad 2/7 and At-Tirmidthi 5/499, see also: *Sahih At-Tirmidthi* 2/155).

"Next, when your bags are packed
And you are all ready to start,

Make sure to take a moment to say
The **Du'a for Traveling** as you **depart**[6]...

It's filled with many wonderful things,
So it takes a little longer to say-

It asks Allah to **help** you on your trip,
And make things **easier** along the way!"

---

[6] Note: The Du'a for Traveling is made at the time of mounting your transport and leaving on a journey.

Du'a for Traveling

اللهُ أَكْبَرُ، اللهُ أَكْبَرُ، اللهُ أَكْبَرُ، سُبْحَانَ الَّذِي سَخَّرَ لَنَا هَذَا وَ مَا كُنَّا لَهُ مُقْرِنِينَ وَ إِنَّا إِلَى رَبِّنَا لَمُنْقَلِبُونَ، اللَّهُمَّ إِنَّا نَسْأَلُكَ فِي سَفَرِنَا هَذَا الْبِرَّ وَ التَّقْوَى، وَ مِنَ الْعَمَلِ مَا تَرْضَى، اللَّهُمَّ هَوِّنْ عَلَيْنَا سَفَرَنَا هَذَا وَاطْوِ عَنَّا بُعْدَهُ، اللَّهُمَّ أَنْتَ الصَّاحِبُ فِي السَّفَرِ، وَ الْخَلِيفَةُ فِي الأَهْلِ، اللَّهُمَّ إِنِّي أَعُوذُ بِكَ مِنْ وَعْثَاءِ السَّفَرِ، وَ كَآبَةِ الْمَنْظَرِ وَ سُوءِ الْمُنْقَلَبِ فِي الْمَالِ وَ الأَهْلِ.

"*Allaahu Akbar, Allaahu Akbar, Allaahu Akbar, Subhaanal-lathee sakh-khara lanaa haathaa wa maa kunnaa lahu muqrineen. Wa innaa ilaa Rabbinaa lamun-qaliboon. Allaahumma innaa nas'aluka fee safarinaa haathal-birra wat-taqwaa, wa minal-'amali maa tardhaa, Allaahumma hawwin 'alaynaa safaranaa haathaa watwi 'annaa bu'dahu, Allaahumma Antas-saahibu fis-safari, wal-khaleefatu fil-ahli, Allaahumma innee a'oothu bika min wa'thaa'is-safari, wa ka'aabatil-mandhari, wa soo'il munqalabi fil-maali wal-ahl[i]."*

(Allah is the greatest, Allah is the greatest, Allah is the greatest, Glory is to Him who has provided this [transport] for us though we could never have had it by our efforts. Surely unto our Lord we are returning. Oh Allah, we ask You on this journey for goodness and piety, and for works that are pleasing to You. Oh Allah, lighten this journey for us and make its distance easy for us. Oh Allah, You are our Companion on the journey and the One in whose care we leave our family, Oh Allah, I seek refuge with You from the difficulties of travel, and from wicked sights and from finding our family and property in misfortune upon returning.)[7]

---

[7] Muslim 2/998

"Then, when you finally get **back home**,
Make the Du'a for Traveling[8] again-

The only difference is that this time,
You add an **extra part** on at the end…"

آيِبُونَ، تَائِبُونَ، عَابِدُونَ، لِرَبِّنَا حَامِدُونَ

"Aa'iboona, taa'iboona, 'aabidoona, li-rabbinaa haamidoon"

(We return, repent, worship and praise our Lord.)

---

[8] Muslim 2/978 (The supplication upon returning from a journey is the same as the supplication when starting a journey, with the additional sentence shown here added on at the end. See "Du'a for Traveling" on the previous page for the first portion of the supplication.)

Tariq practiced hard every day
To make sure that he would know,

All his adi'yaa for traveling
Before it was time for them to go…

When the big day finally came,
Tariq knew exactly what to do-

He remembered to say his adi'yaa
Just as his father had taught him to!

They got on a big red airplane
And took off like they were in a race-

Tariq felt like he was in a rocket
Zooming up into outer space!

Tariq had a great time on the plane
Eating his dinner off a neat little tray,[9]

Then they took out some family games
That they had brought along to play.

---

[9] Note: When traveling in non-Muslim countries, check in advance to assure that the food provided is halal.

After a while Tariq had fallen asleep,
But soon he was wide awake-

As the airplane finally landed,
With a bump, a bounce, and a shake!

His father's family was waiting for them
With laughter, kisses, and smiles-

Then, they were bundled into a car
And driven a few more dusty miles.

They arrived at the large family home,
Cool and shady in the afternoon sun.

Inside they found glasses of sweet juice,
And trays of delicious snacks for everyone!

Tariq spent two wonderful weeks with
His aunts, uncles, cousins, and grandmother-

He had thought he had only one home,
But now he knew he had another!

The day they left was a sad one,
As they got on the airplane again-

He thought of all the people he had met,
And all the interesting places he had been!

Tariq made du'a for those he left behind,[10]
And they made du'a for him, too…

Traveling can be very long and hard,
So it's important to ask Allah to help you!

---

[10] See: "Supplication of the Traveler for the Resident" and "Supplication of the Resident for the Traveler"

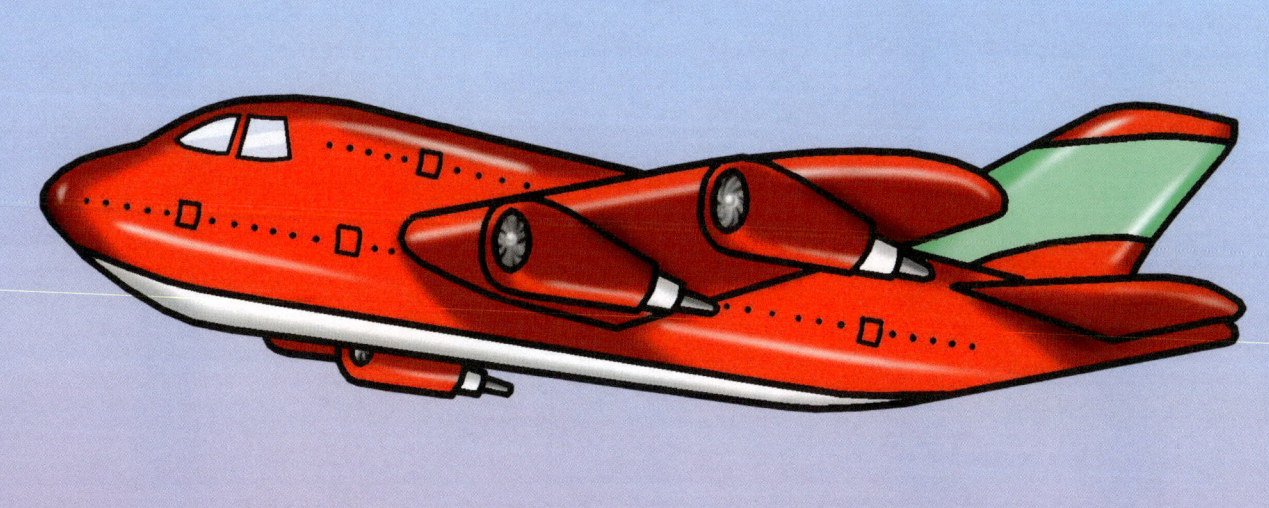

Tariq made du'a again when he got home,
After his long trip traveling all around-

Because it is a **great mercy** from Allah
To arrive back home **safe and sound**!

On your next BIG trip don't forget,
To make your adi'yaa- they're easy to learn;

Always **remember Allah**-
When you **depart** and when you **return**!

Other available titles in the Mini Mu'min Du'a Series:

Batool's Bedtime Story
Bilal's Bakery
Fatimah's First Fasting Day
Jameelah Gets Dressed
Muhammed Goes to the Masjid
Saliha Sneezes
Waheeda the Wudoo' Wonder
Waleed Wakes Up

and many more!...

Visit our online bookstore at:

www.Mini-Mumin.com

Made in the USA
Charleston, SC
13 January 2014